TOTALLY INTO FISHING AND HUNTING

FRESHWATER FISHING

ABBY BADACH DOYLE

Gareth Stevens
PUBLISHING

Please visit our website, www.garethstevens.com. For a free color catalog of all our high-quality books, call toll free 1-800-542-2595 or fax 1-877-542-2596.

Cataloging-in-Publication Data
Names: Doyle, Abby Badach.
Title: Freshwater fishing / Abby Badach Doyle.
Description: New York : Gareth Stevens Publishing, 2023. | Series: Totally into fishing and hunting | Includes glossary and index.
Identifiers: ISBN 9781538280034 (pbk.) | ISBN 9781538280058 (library bound) | ISBN 9781538280041 (6pack) | ISBN 9781538280065 (ebook)
Subjects: LCSH: Fishing–Juvenile literature. | Freshwater fishes–Juvenile literature.
Classification: LCC SH445.D69 2023 | DDC 799.1'1–dc23

Portions of this work were originally authored by Andrea Palmer and published as *We're Going Freshwater Fishing*. All new material in this edition is authored by Abby Badach Doyle.

Published in 2023 by
Gareth Stevens Publishing
29 East 21st Street
New York, NY 10010

Editor: Abby Badach Doyle
Designer: Michael Flynn

Photo credits: Cover, pp. 1 Kletr/Shutterstock.com; series background (camo) Alexvectors/Shutterstock.com; p. 5 Rocksweeper/Shutterstock.com; p. 6 Mintimages/Shutterstock.com; p. 7 Maclane Parker/Shutterstock.com; p. 9 Randy Bjorklund/Shutterstock.com; p. 11 Derek Hatfield/Shutterstock.com; p. 12 NikolayAnikeev/Shutterstock.com; p. 13 Aleksei Isachenko/Shutterstock.com; p. 15 wavebreakmedia/Shutterstock.com; p. 17 MartiRejzek/Shutterstock.com; p. 18 cpaulfell/Shutterstock.com; p. 19 Stephen Mcsweeny/Shutterstock.com; p. 21 sianc/Shutterstock.com; p. 23 Weredragon/Shutterstock.com; p. 24 lauraslens/Shutterstock.com; p. 25 tab62/Shutterstock.com; p. 26 Peyker/Shutterstock.com; p. 27 David Ryznar/Shutterstock.com; p. 29 Kris Wiktor/Shutterstock.com.

Printed in the United States of America

A NOTE TO READERS
Always talk with a parent or teacher before proceeding with any of the activities found in this book. Some activities require adult supervision.

A NOTE TO PARENTS AND TEACHERS
This book was written to be informative and entertaining. Some of the activities in this book require adult supervision. Please talk with your child or student before allowing them to proceed with any hunting activities. The author and publisher specifically disclaim any liability for injury or damages that may result from use of information in this book.

Some of the images in this book illustrate individuals who are models. The depictions do not imply actual situations or events.

CPSIA compliance information: Batch #CSGS23: For further information contact Gareth Stevens, New York, New York at 1-800-542-2595.

Find us on 🇫 📷

CONTENTS

WORDS IN THE GLOSSARY APPEAR IN BOLD TYPE THE
FIRST TIME THEY ARE USED IN THE TEXT.

FISHING IS FUN!

Have you ever stared at a body of water and wondered what was swimming down below? That's part of what's fun about fishing. You get to peek into a whole underwater world!

People have been fishing for food for thousands of years. Today, fishing is a popular sport around the world. Fish live in all kinds of water. Fresh water is water that has almost no salt in it. Bodies of fresh water include lakes, rivers, streams, creeks, and ponds.

KNOW THE FACTS!

Oceans and seas are made up of salt water. This type of water is too salty for humans to drink. Some lakes are saltwater too.

Freshwater fishing is the most common kind of fishing in the United States.

TYPES OF FISH

Most of our world's water is salty. Fresh water makes up only 3 percent of the water on Earth. However, just about half of all the world's species of fish live in fresh water. A species is a group of animals or plants that are the same kind.

Fishing for sport is also called angling.
Fishers can be called anglers.

LARGEMOUTH BASS

Scientists believe there are more than 30,000 species of fish on Earth. In the United States, there are many species of freshwater fish. Common types include perch, bass, catfish, walleye, pike, and trout.

KNOW THE FACTS!

You can find largemouth bass in every U.S. state. They are the most popular type of freshwater game fish. Largemouth bass bite hard and fast. That makes them fun to catch!

ON THE MOVE

Some fish **migrate** between fresh water and salt water. Many fishers enjoy trying to catch them while they're on the move. For example, some salmon are born in fresh water. When they grow older, they swim through streams to the ocean.

After a few years, these salmon swim upstream, or against the flow of a stream or river, to fresh water. Then, they spawn, or lay eggs. One kind of trout, called a steelhead, also migrates from salt water to fresh water. Salmon usually spawn once. Steelhead can spawn several times.

KNOW THE FACTS!

Chinook salmon are also called king salmon. They can grow to be 58 inches (1.5 m) long and weigh more than 120 pounds (54.4 kg)!

In Alaska, the peak season for salmon fishing is May through September.

BASIC FISHING GEAR

Almost all types of fishing require a rod and reel. A reel holds your fishing line. Fishing gear, also called tackle, changes by the type of fishing you plan to do. To catch larger fish, you need a stronger line and bigger hooks. To cast farther away, you need a longer rod.

Lures are things used to get the attention of fish. You might also want weights, sinkers, and bobbers. These let you control how deep your line goes in the water.

KNOW THE FACTS!

If you're new to fishing, a good first stop is your local bait and tackle shop. There, a local fishing **expert** can help you pick out the gear you need.

Tackle boxes make it easy to arrange and sort your gear.

FISHING BAIT

Bait is what you put on your hook to help make fish bite. Lures help draw fish in too. Lures look and move like things fish want to eat. Freshwater fish eat worms, **leeches**, crawfish, crickets, grasshoppers, and small fish called minnows. These all make great bait.

You can buy bait fresh or frozen, or catch it yourself.

KNOW THE FACTS!

After baiting your line, you cast it. This is when you swing your rod and let the hook end plop into the water. Learning to cast takes practice.

The bait you use will change based on the kind of fish you want to catch. Bait can be real or **artificial**, such as plastic earthworms. You can use natural and artificial bait together.

KNOW THE RULES

Most states require adults to buy fishing **licenses**. Fishing licenses cost money. In many states, you need to buy a license starting around age 16. Laws and prices are different in each state. A lifetime license costs more than a one-day pass.

Money from fishing licenses pays for projects that make fishing better. This might include cleaning up pollution, building boat ramps, or stocking. States also set limits for how many fish you can catch and how big they must be to keep. This keeps fish populations healthy.

KNOW THE FACTS!

Some states raise fish in hatcheries, or fish farms. When they grow big enough, hatchery managers release them in popular fishing areas like streams, lakes, or ponds. This is known as "stocking."

Most times, children don't need a license if they are fishing with a licensed adult.

FIND A
GOOD SPOT

If you have family or friends who fish, ask them about their favorite local spots. Two of the best places to find fish are where they hide and where they eat. Fish like to hide away from a current, or fast-moving water. They also hide where predators like birds and bears can't see them.

Places where a stream or river flows into a lake are often good sources of food for fish. Fish also feed where rivers and streams bend. These places make good fishing spots.

KNOW THE FACTS!

Some fishers like to share tips with other fishers. Others work hard to find a good fishing spot and prefer to keep it a secret!

Logs, branches, or rocks make good hiding spots for fish.

17

BY BOAT OR ON LAND?

The simplest way to start fishing is to pick a spot on land. This could be on the banks of a pond, from the dock on a lake, or standing in a stream. To fish from land, all you need is your gear and some **patience**!

KNOW THE FACTS!

Wherever you fish, make sure to clean up your trash. Birds and other wildlife can get tangled in leftover fishing line. Eating sinkers or other tackle can make them sick.

You need to pass a safety class to pilot, or drive, a boat in many states.

Other people prefer to fish from boats. On a boat, you can quickly travel to more fishing spots. You can also fish in deeper water. However, boats can be expensive to buy and

TYPES OF
FISHING BOATS

There are many types of boats for freshwater fishing. Small boats are great for fishing in ponds. Bigger boats work best in lakes or large rivers. There are even special kinds of boats called bass boats made just for bass angling.

Motorboats have engines that make them faster but also loud. Be careful not to scare the fish! Quieter choices include canoes, kayaks, and rowboats. However, these are slower than boats with engines because you need to paddle them.

KNOW THE FACTS!

Canoes and kayaks are long, narrow boats that you paddle to move. Canoes are bigger with more room for people and gear.

For safety, you should always wear a life jacket when fishing from a boat.

21

PONDS AND LAKES

A local pond or lake is a great place for your first fishing trip. They offer many places for fish to hide. The water is still and calm. That makes it easier to tell when you get a bite.

Learning to fish takes practice, but it's fun! You'll learn to tie special knots to **attach** your hook to your line. You will also learn how it feels when a fish bites. When you feel that, quickly pull up your rod to "set" the hook.

KNOW THE FACTS!

The Great Lakes are shared between the United States and Canada. More than 170 species of freshwater fish live there. The two most commonly caught fish are yellow perch and walleye.

THE GREAT LAKES

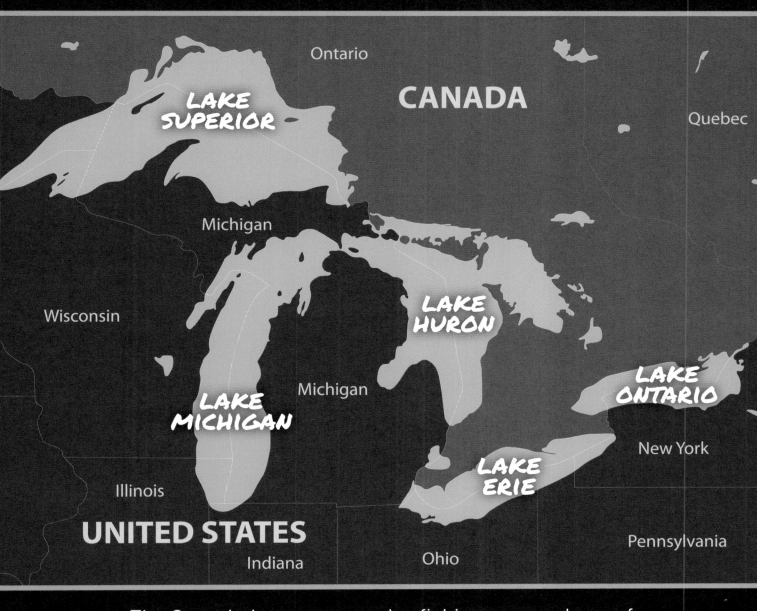

Ontario

CANADA

Quebec

LAKE SUPERIOR

Michigan

Wisconsin

LAKE HURON

LAKE ONTARIO

LAKE MICHIGAN

Michigan

New York

LAKE ERIE

UNITED STATES

Illinois

Indiana

Ohio

Pennsylvania

The Great Lakes are a popular fishing area and one of the largest sources of fresh water in the world.

23

RIVERS AND STREAMS

The water can move quickly in rivers and streams. You need steady footing if you want to stand and fish. Many fishers wear sturdy boots and waterproof bottoms called waders. These go over your clothes like pants or overalls to keep you dry.

KNOW THE FACTS!

A fishing vest has lots of pockets to hold your gear. Pliers are helpful to remove a hook from a fish's mouth. Sunscreen and bug spray are helpful to keep close too.

Many anglers enjoy the art of tying their own flies.

Fly fishing is popular in streams. This form of fishing uses special lures made from hair, string, or feathers to look like flies. You use a special rod and reel to gently snap your line above the water using different methods.

NOODLING AND GIGGING

Not all types of fishing use rods. With noodling, you only use your hands. You swim underwater and use your fingers as bait. Then, you stick your arm right in the mouth of a huge fish! You can get badly hurt while noodling. Not all states allow it.

Gigging is a type of fishing that uses **spears** to stick fish from above. This is a very old form of fishing used by the Ojibwa and other Native Peoples. Usually, gigging happens at night in clear, **shallow** water.

SPEAR

Noodling is popular in the South and Midwest to catch giant catfish.

CAUGHT ONE!

If your fish is large enough, you may be able to keep it to eat. This depends on the species and season. A trusted adult can show you how to clean a fish to prepare it for a meal. Keep fish fresh on crushed ice until you're ready to cook them.

You don't always have to kill your fish, though. Putting fish back is known as catch-and-**release** fishing. Sometimes, enjoying the peace and quiet of nature is satisfying enough.

KNOW THE FACTS!

In catch-and-release fishing, you use smoother hooks that are easier to remove. Then, you unhook the fish gently while it's still

Cook and eat fish right away for the best flavor.

GLOSSARY

artificial: made by people and not by nature

attach: to fix to something

expert: someone who knows a great deal about something

leech: a type of worm that lives in the water and sucks the blood of animals

license: an official paper that gives someone the right to do something

maintain: to care for something by making repairs and changes when needed

migrate: to move from one place to another for feeding or having babies

patience: the ability to wait

release: to set something free

shallow: not deep

spear: a long stick with a sharp point

FOR MORE INFORMATION

BOOKS

Paxton, John. *My Awesome Guide to Freshwater Fishing: Essential Techniques and Tools for Kids.* Emeryville, CA: Rockridge Press, 2021.

Weiner, Andrew. *Down by the River: A Family Fly Fishing Story.* New York, NY: Abrams, 2018.

WEBSITES

Angler Academy for Kids
takemefishing.org/how-to-fish/fishing-resources/angler-academy-for-kids/
Check out crafts, coloring pages, and games all about fishing, and learn where to fish near you.

Fishing by Scout Life
fishing.scoutlife.org
Take a fish-naming quiz and watch videos to learn more about fishing.

INDEX